Desserts
Around the World

Stuffed pancakes (recipe on page 26) are refreshing snacks, especially when served with ice-cold lemonade.

Desserts Around the World

PHOTOGRAPHS BY ROBERT L. AND DIANE WOLFE

easy menu ethnic cookbooks

Lerner Publications Company ▪ Minneapolis

Editor: Mary Winget

The page border for this book is based on vanilla, which is the pod of a climbing orchid plant. Vanilla is used in many parts of the world to enhance the flavors of desserts.

Illustrations by: Laura Westlund, pp. 6, 10, 19, 35; Jeannette Swofford, pp. 25, 27, 31

The photograph on p. 8 is reproduced through the courtesy of Harry J. Lerner, and the photograph on p. 9, Jim Hathaway.

To Eileen Mueller and Theresa Mueller, two of the world's great cooks

Library of Congress Cataloging-in-Publication Data

Desserts around the world / photographs by Robert L. and Diane Wolfe.
     p.   cm. — (Easy menu ethnic cookbooks)
    Includes index.
    Summary: Includes recipes for making the favorite desserts in many countries, from Austria to New Zealand.
    ISBN 0-8225-0926-1
    1. Desserts—Juvenile literature. Hughes, Helga. |1. Desserts. 2. Cookery.| I. Lerner Publications Company. II. Series.
TX773.D4778   1991
641.8′6—dc20
                                 91-11835
                                 CIP
                                 AC

Manufactured in the United States of America

1 2 3 4 5 6 7 8 9 10 99 98 97 96 95 94 93 92 91

The Salzburger sweet soufflé (foreground) is a light Austrian dessert. (Recipe on page 32.)

CONTENTS

NORTH
AMERICA

MEXICO

CARIBBEAN
ISLANDS

SOUTH
AMERICA

BRAZIL

CHILE

ARGENTINA

NORWAY
GERMANY
ENGLAND
EUROPE
FRANCE
ITALY
GREECE

POLAND
AUSTRIA

RUSSIA
(SOVIET UNION)

ASIA

CHINA

LEBANON
ISRAEL

AFRICA

GHANA

KENYA

AUSTRALIA

INTRODUCTION

Dessert, in one form or another, is enjoyed in almost all parts of the world and has been since ancient times. Ancient Egyptians enjoyed eating marzipan made of crushed almonds, and honey provided the basis for many other desserts. In Greece cheesecake was a favorite treat. The Romans ate comparatively simple desserts, such as candied dates stuffed with nuts. During the Dark Ages, people were introduced to fruits and other foods from different areas of Europe and the East when annual fairs were held. By the 14th century, desserts included cakes, rice with almonds and cinnamon, and figs prepared and served in a variety of ways.

Desserts weren't always served at the end of a meal. For many years dessert was served at the same time as the meat or soup. At banquets pastries appeared on the table beside roast goat, cabbage soup, mustard, and pickled cucumbers, and people ate whatever they could reach from where they sat. For a while, desserts were also served between meat courses. Forks weren't invented until the Renaissance, a cultural period that began in Italy in the 14th century and gradually extended throughout the European continent and England. Cooking and table manners became refined, and table settings became elaborate. Dainty cakes with intricate decorations, flavored ice creams and sherbets were served, and such dishes were the beginning of desserts as we currently know them.

While much of the Old World was enjoying rich culinary creations, settlers in the New World were busy trying to find and grow enough food to stay alive. They brought cooking skills and recipes from Europe and learned about new foods and ways to prepare them from the Native Americans. For example, the colonists learned how to grow corn and how to use it in many ways, including the preparation of Indian pudding. They also used apples and wild berries to make pies.

Geography, custom, and a practical use of ingredients are contributing factors to the sweet treats people choose to eat and when they choose to enjoy them. In the past, although main courses were often cooked without recipes, desserts were usually prepared

After dinner, families in the Soviet Union enjoy dessert, coffee, and conversation.

according to a "formula." Many of these formulas were written down and passed from one generation to another, eventually becoming traditional favorites.

Some countries have many different types of food and cooking styles within their own borders. For example, northern and southern Italy are very different from one another. Whereas the north has very fertile land and a large, wealthy population, the south has dry land and a smaller, poorer population. Such differences affect the ingredients available for cooking, and this makes the dishes of northern and southern Italy distinct. In the northern region of Emilia-Romagna, specialities include rich dairy products, and butter is the main cooking fat. In the Tuscany region, where olive trees growing on hillsides replace the fat dairy cows of the north, olive oil is the dominant cooking fat.

In many areas of the world, such as Australia, China, Israel, and the Caribbean, where fruits are plentiful, they are often eaten as dessert, plain or as an important part of a recipe.

In midafternoon many people in Germany and Austria stop work to enjoy *Kaffeetafel,* afternoon coffee and the rich pastries, such as apple cake and Linzer torte, for which those countries are renowned. Light desserts (*Mehlspeisen*), such as sweet soufflés, are served after meals.

In England and Australia, many people stop for tea in the late afternoon. Sometimes it can be quite a formal occasion. Tea is served with a selection of small sandwiches, biscuits, and cakes—both elaborate and plain. Lamingtons (small, frosted cubes of cake covered with coconut) would be a good choice to serve at tea time, and they are a favorite with Australian children.

Sometimes certain desserts are served for particular holidays or for special occasions. In Lebanon, for example, *meghlie*, or milk pudding, is served to visitors when a child is born. Black Forest torte is frequently served for special occasions in Germany. Honey spice cake used to be served during religious holiday celebrations in Russia.

The recipes in this book are from 20 different countries on 6 continents. By making all the recipes, you can sample some of the best taste treats the world has to offer.

This Nigerian woman is selling fruit at an open market. Fruit is a part of many desserts.

BEFORE YOU BEGIN

Cooking any dish, plain or fancy, is easier and more fun if you are familiar with its ingredients. The international dishes in this book make use of some ingredients you may not know. You should also be familiar with the special terms that will be used in these recipes. Therefore, *before* you start cooking, study the following "dictionary" of special ingredients and terms very carefully. Then read through the recipe you want to try from beginning to end.

Now you are ready to shop for ingredients and to organize the cookware you will need. Once you have assembled everything, you can begin to cook. It is also very important to read *The Careful Cook* on page 48 before you start. Following these rules will make your cooking experience safe, fun, and easy.

COOKING UTENSILS

pastry brush— A small brush used for coating food with melted butter or other liquids

rolling pin— A cylindrical tool used for rolling out dough

sieve— A hand-held device with very small holes or fine netting used for draining food or forcing small particles from larger pieces of food

slotted spoon— A spoon with small openings in the bowl. It is used to pick solid food out of a liquid.

spatula— A flat, thin utensil used to lift, toss, scrape, or scoop up food

springform pan — A pan with a detachable rim

COOKING TERMS

beat— To stir rapidly in a circular motion

cream— To beat two or more ingredients together until the mixture is smooth

flute— To create a design around the edge of pie pastry by pinching the pastry gently between your thumb and forefinger

fold—To blend one ingredient with other ingredients by using a gentle overturning circular motion instead of by stirring or beating

garnish—To add a decorative touch

preheat—To allow an oven to warm up to a certain temperature before putting food into it

sauté—To fry in a small amount of oil or fat, stirring or turning the food to prevent burning

scald—To heat a liquid (such as milk) to a temperature just below its boiling point

sift—To mix several dry ingredients together or to remove lumps in dry ingredients by putting them through a sieve or sifter

simmer—To cook over low heat in liquid kept just below boiling point. Bubbles will occasionally rise to the surface.

whip—To beat an ingredient, such as cream or egg white, until light and fluffy

SPECIAL INGREDIENTS

almond extract—A liquid made from the oil of the almond nut and used to give an almond flavor to food

cardamom—A spice from the ginger family that has a rich aroma and gives food a sweet, cool taste

cream of tartar—A white, powdery substance often used in baking

gelatin—A clear, powdered substance used as a thickening agent

kiwifruit—A small, oval fruit with fuzzy, brown skin covering bright green flesh marked with a circle of tiny, black seeds

mango—A greenish yellow tropical fruit with soft, juicy, yellow flesh

orange flower water—A liquid flavoring made from distilled orange blossoms

phyllo—Paper-thin dough used in many Greek recipes. Phyllo is available frozen at many supermarkets and at specialty stores.

poppy seed filling—A thick, sweet mixture made from poppy seeds and corn syrup used in making cakes, pies, and breads

vermicelli—Pasta made in long, thin strands that are thinner than spaghetti

yeast—An ingredient used in baking that causes dough to rise

AN INTERNATIONAL DESSERT MENU

Below is a menu of desserts from many parts of the world. The ethnic names of the dishes are given, along with a guide on how to pronounce them.

ENGLISH NAME	ETHNIC NAME/ PRONUNCIATION GUIDE	COUNTRY
Vermicelli and Raisins		Kenya
Sweet Balls		Ghana
Glazed Kiwi Tart		Australia
Lamingtons		Australia
Almond Fruit Float		China
Poppy Seed Cake	Ugat Pereg (oo-GAHT PAY-reg)	Israel
Melon Dessert	Liftan Melon (lif-TAHN meh-LONE)	Israel
Stuffed Pancakes	Atayef Meshi (ah-TAH-yef MEH-shee)	Lebanon
Walnut-Honey Pastry	Baklava (bah-klah-VAH)	Greece
Sacher Cake	Sacher Torte (ZAHK-er TOHR-teh)	Austria
Salzburger Sweet Soufflé	Salzburger Nockerln (SAHLZ-bohr-ger NOK-erln)	Austria
Summer Pudding		England
Pears Helen	Poires Helene (pwahr ay-LEN)	France

ENGLISH NAME	ETHNIC NAME/ PRONUNCIATION GUIDE	COUNTRY
Apple Cake	Schlupfkucken (SHLOOPF-koo-ken)	Germany
Biscuit Tortoni	Tortoni (tor-TOH-nee)	Italy
Honey Spice Cake	Kovrizhka Medovaya (kov-RISH-kah meh-DOH-vah-yah)	Russia
Fruit Soup	Fruktsuppe (FRUKT-suh-puh)	Norway
Semi-Shortbread with Plums or Apricots	Placek Pótkruchy ze Sliwkami lub z Morelami (PLAH-tsek poow-KROO-hih zeh-sheef-KAH-mee loop zmoh-reh-LAH-mee)	Poland
Mango with Cinnamon	Mango canela (MAHN-goh kah-NAY-lah)	Mexico
Coconut Ice		Barbados
Banana Fritters		Caribbean Islands
Almond Meringue with Fresh Fruit		Chile
Milk Pudding	Dulce le Leche (DOOL-thay day LAY-chay)	Brazil
Filled Cookies	Alfoyores (al-fah-YOH-rays)	Argentina

Like most African desserts, vermicelli and raisins (*front*) and sweet balls (*back right*) are light and tasty and not very sweet.

Ghana is located in West Africa, and Kenya is in East Africa. Because food is often scarce in certain parts of Africa, East and West African cooks have learned to work with whatever they have. Most African dishes are versatile enough to substitute one ingredient for another. The following two recipes, which require only a few basic ingredients, are best when they are served warm.

Sweet Balls
Ghana

Recipe by Constance Nabwire and Bertha Vining Montgomery

  1 **egg**
  ½ **teaspoon salt**
  3 **tablespoons baking powder**
1½ **cups sugar**
  ½ **teaspoon nutmeg**
1½ **cups warm water**
3¾ **to 4¼ cups all-purpose flour**
    vegetable oil

1. In a large bowl, combine egg, salt, baking powder, sugar, and nutmeg, and stir well. Add 1½ cups warm water and stir again.
2. Gradually stir in enough flour so that dough is stiff and only slightly sticky.
3. With clean, floured hands, roll dough into balls the size of walnuts.
4. Pour ½ inch oil into pan and heat over medium-high heat for 4 to 5 minutes.
5. Carefully place balls in oil, a few at a time, and fry 3 or 4 minutes per side or until golden brown. Remove from pan with slotted spoon and drain on paper towel. Serve warm.

Makes 25 to 30 doughnuts

Vermicelli and Raisins
Kenya

Recipe by Constance Nabwire and Bertha Vining Montgomery

2 tablespoons vegetable oil
2 cups vermicelli, broken into 1-inch pieces
2 cups hot water
¾ teaspoon ground cardamom
¼ cup sugar
¼ cup raisins
¼ cup chopped dates
¼ cup chopped walnuts

1. In a large frying pan, heat oil over medium heat for 1 minute. Add vermicelli and sauté until light brown.
2. Slowly add 2 cups hot water. Stir in cardamom, sugar, raisins, dates, and nuts.
3. Cover, reduce heat to low, and simmer over medium-low heat, stirring occasionally, for about 10 minutes or until all water is absorbed and vermicelli is tender.

Serves 4 to 6

Glazed Kiwi Tart
Australia

Recipe by Elizabeth Germaine and
Ann L. Burckhardt

*The kiwifruit, from New Zealand, is named
for the kiwi bird. It has a delicious, mixed-
fruit flavor and is high in vitamin C.*

Pastry:

**1 9-inch unbaked pie shell (can be
purchased in the refrigerated
section of supermarkets)**

1. Follow the directions for a one-crust pie.
Using a knife or kitchen shears, trim off
any pastry that's hanging over the edge of
the pie plate; flute the edge.
2. With a fork, prick thoroughly the bottom
and sides of the pastry shell.
3. Bake according to package directions.

Filling:

**1 8-ounce cream cheese, at
room temperature**

**⅔ cup sugar
1½ teaspoons vanilla extract
3 tablespoons heavy cream
3 ripe kiwifruit**

1. Stir together the cream cheese, sugar,
and vanilla, and cream until smooth.
Spread the cream cheese filling in the
cooled pastry shell.
2. Peel the kiwifruit with a paring knife.
Slice the fruit into thin slices. Arrange the
slices on top of the cream cheese filling,
overlapping them in circles.

Glaze:

**¼ cup apricot preserves
1 tablespoon water**

1. Combine the preserves and water in
a small saucepan and heat until preserves
melt. Cool the glaze slightly, stirring
occasionally. Spoon the glaze over the
kiwifruit. Chill the tart until ready to serve.
Serves 6 to 8

Glazed kiwi tart, an easy-to-make dessert, provides a colorful finale to dinner, and it is also high in vitamin C.

Lamingtons are a teatime favorite among Australian children.

Lamingtons
Australia

Recipe by Elizabeth Germaine and
Ann L. Burckhardt

*These popular cakes are named in honor of
Baroness Lamington, wife of the governor of
Queensland at the turn of the century. They
are a favorite with Australian children.*

Cake:

**1 (two-layer-size) package of yellow
cake mix**

1. Bake cake as directed on the package for
a 9- by 13-inch cake. Cool cake on a wire
rack.
2. Trim crusts off the cooled cake. Cut
cake into 2½-inch squares.

Icing:

3 cups powdered sugar
⅓ cup cocoa
3 tablespoons butter or margarine,
**   melted**
½ cup boiling water
**   About 3 cups shredded coconut**

1. Sift powdered sugar and cocoa into a bowl. Add the melted butter and boiling water; mix well until smooth.
2. Stand the icing bowl in a saucepan of simmering water, about ¼ full.
3. Place the coconut in a shallow bowl next to the pan. Place a wire rack on the other side of the coconut, so that you have a lamington assembly line.

4. Using two forks, dip each square of cake into the hot icing. Let the excess icing drip off. Then put the icing-covered cake in the coconut. Using two other forks, roll the cake in the coconut to cover it on all 6 sides. Place the lamingtons on the wire rack. When they are all iced, put them in a cool place until the icing hardens. Store any leftover cakes in an airtight container.

Makes 12 individual cakes

Almond Fruit Float
China

Recipe by Ling Yu

The Chinese eat very few desserts. Usually they end a meal with fresh fruit. Pastries and sweet dishes are made in China, but they are special festival foods and are rarely served with the daily meal. In the West, people often end a Chinese meal with fortune cookies. Like chop suey, however, these cookies are unknown in China. In this recipe, any kind of fruit, fresh or canned, may be used. Mandarin oranges, sliced peaches, fruit cocktail, and pineapple make delicious floats.

1 envelope unflavored gelatin
1 cup water
½ cup sugar
½ cup milk
1 tablespoon almond extract
1 13-ounce can fruit with syrup

1. In a saucepan, dissolve gelatin in water. Place over high heat and bring to a boil. Then reduce heat to low.
2. Add sugar and stir until thoroughly dissolved.
3. Stir in milk and almond extract. Mix well.
4. Pour into a deep, square pan and allow to set at room temperature. Then put in refrigerator to cool.
5. When cool, cut into cubes and serve topped with fruit and syrup. (If there is not enough syrup with the fruit, make a syrup by mixing 1 cup of water with 3 tablespoons sugar and ¼ teaspoon almond extract. Chill and serve with fruit and gelatin.)

Serves 6

Almond fruit float can be made with either fresh or canned fruit.

Melon Dessert/
Liftan Melon
Israel

Recipe by Josephine Bacon

Israel is a country with a very unusual heritage. It is the ancient land of the Bible, the setting for the events described in the scriptures sacred to both Jews and Christians. The food of Israel is as unique as its history. It is a blend of many different cooking traditions, combining Middle Eastern and European influences with a uniquely Jewish flavor. Fruits and vegetables, which are abundant and inexpensive, can be found at nearly every meal. Israeli melons are small cantaloupe-style melons called Ogen melons. They are named for the kibbutz *where they were first grown.*

2 small cantaloupes
½ pound green grapes
½ pound red grapes
4 peaches

This melon dessert is a simple, yet festive, way to end a meal.

1 teaspoon cinnamon
1 cup white grape juice

1. Cut melons in half. Scrape out and discard seeds. Scrape out most of the melon flesh, being careful not to pierce the skin.
2. With a melon baller, cut melon flesh into small balls, or cut it into small pieces with a sharp knife.
3. Wash grapes and remove from stems. (If grapes have seeds, cut in half and discard seeds.) Save four tiny clusters of red grapes for decoration.
4. Half fill a medium saucepan with water and bring to a boil over high heat. Carefully place peaches into boiling water. After 5 minutes, remove them with a slotted spoon. When peaches are cool enough to handle, peel and cut into small pieces.
5. In a large bowl, combine cinnamon, grape juice, melon, grapes, and peaches, and stir. Spoon mixture back into melon shells. Top with reserved grape clusters. Refrigerate and serve cold.

Serves 4

Poppy seed cake can be made with either prune or poppy seed filling. (Recipe on page 24.)

Poppy Seed Cake
Ugat Pereg
Israel

Recipe by Josephine Bacon

In Israel, one can always expect company, invited or not, after the Friday evening meal. This is a good cake to have on hand to serve visitors. A 12-ounce can of prune filling can be substituted for the poppy seed filling. (If you use one of the new quick-acting yeasts, follow package directions instead of the instructions given here.)

Cake:

½ **cup milk**
1 **envelope active dry yeast**
1 **tablespoon sugar**
2 **cups all-purpose flour, plus extra for rolling dough**
½ **cup butter or margarine, softened**
1 **12-ounce can poppy seed filling**

1. In a small saucepan, scald milk over low heat. Remove from heat and let cool slightly.
2. Warm a small cup or bowl by rinsing in hot water and drying thoroughly. In warmed bowl, combine yeast with 1 teaspoon sugar and 1 tablespoon flour. Add warm milk and stir until dissolved. Cover with a cloth and leave in a warm place for about 20 minutes or until mixture foams.
3. In a large bowl, beat together butter and remaining sugar until smooth. Gradually add remaining flour, beating constantly. Stir in yeast mixture.
4. Place dough on floured wooden board or countertop. Knead for about 15 minutes, adding enough flour to produce an elastic dough that is no longer sticky.
5. Wash out bowl with hot water, dry thoroughly, and grease. Return dough to bowl, cover with plastic wrap, and leave in a warm place to rise for 1 hour. (This is a rather dry dough and will not rise much.)
6. Sprinkle wooden board or countertop with more flour. With a floured rolling pin, roll out dough into an 8- by 10-inch rectangle. Spread poppy seed filling evenly

over dough, leaving a margin of about ½ inch around edges. Starting at one of the long sides, roll up dough jelly-roll fashion.
7. Grease cookie sheet. Slide cake carefully onto the cookie sheet, turning it so the seam is underneath to keep filling from escaping during baking. Cover cake with a damp kitchen towel and leave in a warm place for 1 hour.
8. Preheat oven to 400°
9. Uncover cake and bake for 10 minutes. Then reduce heat to 375° and bake for 30 minutes or until golden brown.
10. Remove cake from oven and let cool completely before transferring to a wire rack.

Frosting:

2 cups powdered sugar
1 egg white, lightly beaten
½ teaspoon lemon juice
¼ to ½ cup water

1. Sift powdered sugar into a medium mixing bowl. Make a well in the center of sugar and pour egg white and lemon juice into it. Gradually mix powdered sugar into liquid with a spoon, adding water little by little until frosting is smooth. (Frosting should be thick enough to coat the back of a spoon.)
2. When completely smooth, pour frosting over cake, letting it dribble down the sides.

Makes about 30 slices

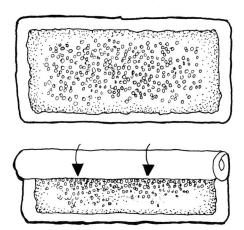

Stuffed Pancakes/ Atayef Mehshi
Lebanon

Recipe by Suad Amari

These delicious pancakes are sold in the souk, or street market, in the winter. They are eaten by Lebanese Muslims on all festive occasions, especially after the month-long fast of Ramadan, which is the equivalent of Christianity's Lent. Although the flavor and texture will not be the same, you can simplify the recipe by substituting any pancake mix for the batter recipe.

Filling:

2 **cups chopped walnuts**
3 **tablespoons sugar**
2 **teaspoons cinnamon**

Syrup:

1 **cup pancake syrup or dark corn syrup**
½ **tablespoon orange flower water (optional)**

Batter:

1 **envelope active dry yeast**
1 **teaspoon sugar**
1¼ **to 2 cups lukewarm water**
1½ **cups all-purpose flour**
½ **cup vegetable oil (for frying)**

1. Dissolve yeast and sugar in ½ cup warm water. Cover lightly with a damp cloth and leave in a warm place for about 20 minutes or until mixture begins to foam.
2. In a small bowl, mix walnuts, sugar, and cinnamon. Set aside.
3. In another small bowl, combine syrup and orange flower water. Set aside.
4. Warm a large mixing bowl by rinsing with hot water and drying thoroughly. Sift flour into warmed bowl. Make a depression in the center, pour in yeast mixture, and beat into the flour. Continue beating, gradually adding water until mixture is the consistency of pancake batter.
5. Cover mixture with a damp cloth and leave in a warm place for 1 hour or until bubbly.
6. Heat a heavy skillet or omelette pan over

high heat. When hot, add 1 teaspoon oil and swirl to coat skillet evenly.

7. Pour ¼ cup batter into pan. Tilt pan gently to even out batter, but keep pancake fairly thick and round. Cook until it begins to bubble and comes away easily from pan. Cook only one side of pancake. Repeat with remaining batter, adding oil to pan as needed.

8. Put 2 tablespoons filling on uncooked side of each pancake and fold in half. Pinch edges together firmly to keep filling in place.

9. Pour 2 tablespoons oil into skillet and fry folded pancakes about 2 to 3 minutes on each side or until golden brown. (Add more oil as needed.) Drain well on paper towels.

10. Dip pancakes in syrup mixture while they are still warm and serve with sour cream or cottage cheese.

Serves 4 to 6

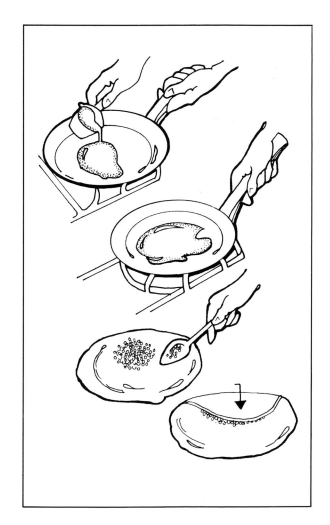

Layer upon layer of flaky, buttery phyllo, nutmeg-spiced walnuts and almonds, and a sweet honey sauce make *baklavá* an unforgettable treat. (Recipe on page 30.)

WORKING WITH PHYLLO

Phyllo (FEE-low) dough is paper-thin dough made of flour and water. It is used with various fillings for many Greek dishes. Phyllo dough is available frozen in many supermarkets and in specialty stores. Each sheet is brushed well with melted butter before baking. This makes the phyllo turn light, flaky, golden, and delicious.

Phyllo is extremely fragile, but using it is not difficult if you follow these basic rules:

1. Thaw frozen phyllo in its original package for 24 hours in the refrigerator.
2. Do not unwrap phyllo until you are ready to use it. Make sure your work area is cleared, your melted butter and pastry brush are ready, and your filling is prepared.
3. Remove rings from your fingers and make sure your fingernails are not too long. (Fingernails can tear the phyllo.)
4. Work with one sheet at a time. Peel sheets carefully from package.
5. After removing a sheet, cover remaining sheets tightly with either plastic wrap or a slightly damp kitchen towel (not terry cloth).
6. Leftover phyllo will stay fresh in the refrigerator for 1 week if covered well with plastic wrap.
7. If phyllo is not available where you live, you can substitute frozen puff pastry, thawed and rolled very thin with a rolling pin. It won't be as thin as phyllo, though, so use 1 or 2 fewer layers than called for in a recipe.

Walnut-Honey Pastry/ Baklavá
Greece
Recipe by Lynne W. Villios

When one thinks of Greece, what often comes to mind is the ancient civilization that flourished there thousands of years ago. The art of cooking was appreciated even then. In fact, the world's first cookbook is said to have been written in 350 B.C. by the philosopher Archestratus. At that time, cooks were very highly regarded and thought of as artists. Because Greece is located between western Europe and the Middle East, Greek cooking reflects the influences of both areas. Climate also influences Greek cuisine. Honey, which is found wild in all parts of Greece, is the favorite sweetener, and it is often used in the many sweet pastries Greeks enjoy. Baklavá is no doubt the best known of these, and it is the favorite Greek dessert. The pastry is made with phyllo dough, so read over the instructions on page 29 for tips on working with the fragile phyllo sheets.

Syrup:

  1 cup sugar
  1 cup water
1½-inch-thick slice lemon
  1 stick cinnamon
  1 cup honey

1. In a small saucepan, combine sugar, water, lemon slice, and cinnamon stick.
2. Bring to a boil over medium heat. Reduce heat and simmer 10 minutes.
3. Remove pan from heat. Stir in honey and cool thoroughly.
4. When cool, remove the lemon slice and cinnamon stick.

Pastry:

  4 cups (1 pound) finely ground walnuts
  2 cups (½ pound) finely ground blanched or unblanched almonds
  ¼ cup sugar
  2 teaspoons cinnamon

½ teaspoon nutmeg
1½ cups (3 sticks) butter or margarine, melted
1 1-pound package phyllo pastry, thawed

1. Preheat oven to 300°.
2. In a large bowl, combine walnuts, almonds, sugar, cinnamon, and nutmeg.
3. Grease a 9- by 13-inch pan with 2 tablespoons butter.
4. Place 4 sheets of phyllo in the pan, brushing each with melted butter before adding the next. Butter the fourth sheet also.
5. Sprinkle ½ to ¾ cup of nut mixture over the phyllo.
6. Top nut mixture with 2 more sheets of phyllo, buttering each sheet well.
7. Continue alternating nut mixture with 2 sheets buttered phyllo until both are used up, ending with phyllo. Brush top with butter.
8. With a sharp knife, trim off any excess phyllo on the sides of the pastry.
9. With a sharp knife, make 1½-inch-wide lengthwise cuts in the dough. (Do not cut all the way through the dough. Cut through the top layer only.)
10. Then make 1½-inch diagonal cuts to create diamond-shaped pieces. (Again, cut through the top layer only.)
11. Bake baklavá for 1 hour or until golden brown.
12. Remove from oven and place on a cooling rack.
13. Cut through diamonds completely with a sharp knife. Immediately pour the cooled syrup over hot pastry.
14. Cool and serve on dessert plates.

Makes about 3 dozen pieces

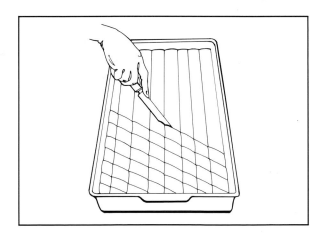

Salzburger Sweet Soufflé
Salzburger Nockerln
Austria

Recipe by Helga Hughes

Throughout Austrian history, different groups of people settled in the country, and each group brought its own customs and cuisine. As the various groups mixed, they helped shape Austrian culture. This blend of cultures adds to the variety and flavor of many Austrian dishes.

After meals, Austrians serve light desserts (Mehlspeisen), such as sweet soufflés, rather than rich pastries. This soufflé, the lightest of desserts, is a perfect ending for a festive dinner.

4 eggs, separated
⅛ teaspoon vanilla extract
½ teaspoon lemon peel, grated
2 tablespoons flour
2 tablespoons sugar
2 tablespoons butter

1. Preheat oven to 350°.
2. In a bowl, stir together egg yolks, vanilla, and grated lemon peel, then sift flour over mixture.
3. In another bowl, beat egg whites with 1 tablespoon sugar until stiff.
4. Using a rubber spatula, fold egg whites into egg yolk mixture.
5. Generously butter a baking dish and place four equal parts of the mixture side by side in the dish. Sprinkle lightly with remaining sugar, then bake on middle rack of oven for 12 to 15 minutes—until the soufflé is lightly browned on the outside but still soft inside. Remove from oven and serve immediately.

Serves 4

Vienna, Austria, is renowned for its delicious pastries. The Sacher Torte (*foreground*) is probably the city's most famous cake. (Recipe on page 34.)

Sacher Cake/ Sacher Torte
Austria

Recipe by Helga Hughes

Viennese Prince Klemens von Metternich is partially responsible for bringing us the Sachertorte, one of Austria's most famous cakes. Created in 1832 by master baker Franz Sacher to please the prince, the cake soon gained popularity. Later, descendants of the master baker built and operated the Sacher Hotel in Vienna and made this delicious cake their specialty. When a popular Viennese pastry shop copied the recipe, the Sachers took them to court. A decision worthy of Solomon resulted from the much-publicized trial: the Sachers would retain their rights under the name Sachertorte, *while others would be required to call their copies* Sacher Torte. *This delicious cake is often served with whipped cream.*

Cake:

5⅓ ounces bittersweet chocolate
1 stick plus 3 tablespoons butter, melted
½ cup sugar
6 eggs, separated
1 tablespoon powdered sugar
1 cup flour
1 tablespoon baking powder
12 ounces apricot jam at room temperature

1. Prepare a 9-inch springform pan by cutting waxed paper the exact size of the base of the pan, plus a 29- by 2¼-inch strip for the sides. (Measure the circle for the base by putting the pan on top of the waxed paper and drawing a circle around it.) Insert waxed paper in pan.
2. Preheat oven to 325°.
3. In a double boiler, heat the chocolate until melted.
4. In a large bowl, beat butter and sugar. Add melted chocolate, then add egg yolks, one at a time, beating continuously to make a creamy mixture.
5. In another bowl, using clean beaters,

beat egg whites and powdered sugar until stiff peaks form.

6. Add egg whites to chocolate mixture, then sift baking powder and flour together onto egg whites, a little at a time. Fold egg whites and flour carefully into chocolate mixture.

7. Pour into prepared pan, spreading batter evenly. Bake for about 50 minutes. (Test for doneness by inserting a toothpick into cake. If the toothpick comes out clean, the cake is done.)

8. Remove cake from oven, remove spring-form rim, carefully peel off side paper, and allow cake to cool slightly.

9. Turn onto a cake plate and remove base of pan and waxed paper. Slice cake horizontally, spread bottom layer with jam, and replace top layer.

Chocolate Icing:

7 ounces bittersweet chocolate
1 cup powdered sugar
2 tablespoons butter
8 to 10 tablespoons hot water and a few drops fresh lemon juice

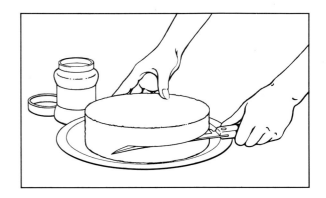

1. Melt chocolate in double boiler.

2. Add powdered sugar, butter, lemon juice, and hot water—a tablespoon at a time—to get right consistency for spreading on cake. While icing is still hot, spread over top and sides of cake and allow icing to cool completely.

Serves 12

Serve pears Helen in glass dishes to show off its colorful layers.

Pears Helen/
Poires Hélène
France

Recipe by Lynne Marie Waldee

French cooks, who consider cooking a fine art, bring out the flavors in foods and serve food in the most attractive way possible.

½ cup chocolate syrup
4 to 8 scoops vanilla ice cream
4 canned pear halves, drained
⅓ cup raspberry or strawberry jam
1 tablespoon hot water

1. In the bottom of each of 4 sherbet glasses or bowls, put 2 tablespoons chocolate syrup.
2. On top of syrup, place 1 or 2 scoops of ice cream.
3. Place 1 pear half, cut side down, on top of each portion of ice cream.
4. Combine jam and water in a separate bowl and spoon mixture over each pear.

Serves 4

Biscuit Tortoni/ Tortoni
Italy

Recipe by Alphonse Bisignano

¾ cup chilled whipping cream
3 tablespoons sugar
½ cup almond macaroon cookie crumbs
1 teaspoon almond extract
2 tablespoons chopped maraschino cherries
¼ cup chopped toasted almonds

1. Line 6 muffin or custard cups with paper cupcake liners.
2. Beat whipping cream and sugar in a chilled bowl until stiff.
3. Set aside 2 tablespoons macaroon crumbs. Fold rest of crumbs, almond extract, cherries, and almonds into whipped cream.
4. Spoon mixture into prepared cups and sprinkle with remaining crumbs. Cover with plastic wrap and freeze until firm.

Serves 6

Biscuit tortoni is a sweet dessert that is very easy to prepare.

Apple Cake/ Schlupfkucken Germany

Recipe by Helga Parnell

Germany has long been known for its delicious cuisine. Besides the freshest ingredients, German cooks add love, time, patience, and imagination to their recipes. The result is always delectable. In this recipe, you can substitute one pound of cherries, pitted, for the apples.

Apple cake is a dessert commonly served with afternoon coffee.

1⅓ cup all-purpose flour
1¼ teaspoon baking powder
¼ pound (½ cup) margarine, softened
½ cup plus 2 tablespoons sugar
2 eggs at room temperature
  rind of ½ lemon, grated
  lemon juice from one lemon
6 small tart apples
2 teaspoons cinnamon

1. Preheat oven to 350°. Grease a 10-inch springform pan.

2. In a medium bowl, combine flour and baking powder.

3. In a large bowl, cream together margarine and ½ cup sugar. Add eggs and lemon rind and blend until fluffy. Add flour mixture stir well, and then pour into pan.

4. Squeeze lemon juice into a small bowl. Peel and core apples and cut into quarters. Dip pieces of apple into lemon juice so they won't turn brown as you work with them. Make deep lengthwise cuts at ⅛-inch intervals across rounded side of each piece of apple.

5. Press apples, cut side up, into the dough.

6. In a small bowl, combine cinnamon with 2 tablespoons sugar. Sprinkle evenly over apples.

7. Bake for 30 to 40 minutes or until toothpick inserted in center of cake (not in apple) comes out clean.

8. Serve with whipped cream.

Makes 8 to 10 pieces

Apples or pears make good substitutes in semi-shortbread if fresh plums or apricots are not available. (Recipe on page 41.)

Summer Pudding
England

Recipe by Barbara W. Hill

Summer pudding is especially good when made with fresh fruit. Just use 1 cup fresh raspberries, 1 cup fresh, sliced strawberries, and 2 cups fresh blackberries. Sweetened frozen fruit can also be used, but remember to omit the 1 cup of sugar.

1 **10-ounce package frozen unsweetened raspberries, thawed**
1 **10-ounce package frozen unsweetened sliced strawberries, thawed**
1 **1-pound package frozen unsweetened blackberries, thawed**
1 **cup sugar**
1 **loaf sliced white bread, several days old**

1. Stir all fruit and sugar together in a large bowl. (Allow frozen fruit to defrost thoroughly.)
2. Meanwhile, cut the crusts off as many bread slices as you will need to line a deep 2-quart bowl. Cut a round piece for the bottom of the bowl and several overlapping wedges for the sides.
3. Line the bowl with bread and pour in fruit mixture and juices. Cover the top completely with more bread slices.
4. Over top bread slices, put a plate that is small enough to fit inside the rim of the bowl. Place a heavy weight, such as a brick or a rock, on top to press it down firmly. Refrigerate for at least 24 hours.
5. When ready to serve, remove the weight and plate. To unmold pudding, place a serving plate upside down on top of the bowl. Then, grasping plate and bowl firmly, turn them over quickly. The pudding should slide easily onto the plate. If it doesn't, slide a knife blade around the inside edge of the bowl to loosen it.
6. The fruit juices should now be soaked up by the bread so that the pudding is a rich purple-red color. Serve with a large bowl of fresh whipped cream.

Serves 8

Semi-Shortbread with Plums or Apricots
Poland

Recipe by Danuta Zamojska-Hutchins

Dough:

2 cups all-purpose flour
1½ teaspoons baking powder
½ cup powdered sugar
½ teaspoon salt
4 ounces (½ cup) sour cream
**¼ cup (½ stick) butter or margarine,
    softened**
1 egg, lightly beaten
1 egg yolk

Topping:

1 pound fresh purple plums or apricots
¼ cup powdered sugar
½ cup sour cream
1 teaspoon vanilla or almond extract
¼ to ½ cup powdered sugar for sprinkling

1. Preheat oven to 375°. Then grease and flour a 9- by 13-inch baking pan.

2. Wash plums, cut in half lengthwise, and remove stems and pits.
3. In a mixing bowl, make topping by blending together powdered sugar, sour cream, and vanilla.
4. In another bowl, mix together flour, baking powder, powdered sugar, and salt.
5. Cut butter into small pieces and add to flour mixture. Mash with a fork until well blended. Mixture should resemble large bread crumbs.
6. Add egg, egg yolk, and sour cream to flour mixture and mix well with your hands until smooth.
7. Spread dough evenly on bottom of pan.
8. Place plum halves skin side down on dough and press into dough. (Make sure there is some dough showing around each plum.) Put 1 teaspoon topping on each plum half.
9. Put on middle oven rack and bake 30 minutes or until golden brown.
10. Put powdered sugar in flour sifter and sift over plums. Cut into squares to serve.

Makes 18 to 24 squares

Cinnamon sticks add a spicy tang to Norwegian fruit soup.

Fruit Soup/ Fruktsuppe
Norway

Recipe by Sylvia Munson

If you look at a map, you will see that Norway is shaped like a spoon. This is fitting because Norway is known for its use of many different types of food, all of which are attractively prepared. You might find this fruit soup at a Norwegian smorgasbord (SMOER-gus-boerd), a buffet of many different dishes. The soup is cool, spicy, and refreshing.

1-pound package unpitted prunes
½ pound (1½ cups) raisins
2 cinnamon sticks
6 cups water
4 ounces (1 cup) dried apricots
1 8¾-ounce can unsweetened cherries
    and juice
3 tablespoons quick-cooking tapioca
¼ cup sugar

1. Put prunes, raisins, cinnamon sticks, and water in a large, heavy kettle. Bring to a boil, then reduce heat and simmer about 30 minutes or until prunes and raisins are soft.
2. Add apricots and cook for 10 minutes or until they are plump and soft.
3. Pour off liquid from cooked fruit into another kettle. (You may need help from a friend when you do this.) Add juice from cherries to liquid. Then add tapioca and sugar. Cook over medium heat, stirring often, until tapioca is clear. The juice should be thick by this time. (You will have to cook mixture for at least 30 minutes to get clear tapioca and thickened juice.)
4. Add thickened juice and cherries to fruit. Stir. You can add slices of oranges and lemons to this mixture for color. Serve while warm, or eat cold.

Serves 12

Honey Spice Cake/ Kovrizhka Medovaya Russia

Recipe by Gregory and Rita Plotkin

Russia is what many people call the country whose official name is the Union of Soviet Socialist Republics (USSR). Russia is the USSR's largest republic. The USSR is a union of people of many different ethnic backgrounds and even different languages. The cuisine of the USSR is as varied and interesting as its people. Honey spice cake used to be served during religious holiday celebrations in Russia. Now it is a common dessert that is especially popular with children.

2 eggs
½ cup brown sugar
2 cups all-purpose flour
½ teaspoon baking soda
1 cup honey
½ cup raisins
½ cup sliced almonds (or other nuts)

1. Grease and flour a 9- by 5-inch loaf pan. Preheat oven to 350°.
2. Beat eggs thoroughly in a small bowl. Add sugar and stir well.
3. Pour flour into a large mixing bowl. Add egg mixture and baking soda and stir well.
4. Add honey and mix for 10 minutes. Stir in raisins.
5. Pour dough into pan, level it out, and sprinkle with nuts.
6. Bake for 50 to 60 minutes or until toothpick stuck in the middle of cake comes out clean.
7. Serve with whipped cream or jam.

Makes 9 to 12 pieces

Mango with Cinnamon/ Mango Canela
Mexico

Recipe by Rosa Coronado

Today most Mexicans are descended from both Spanish and Indian ancestors. The food of Mexico is a blend of those two rich traditions. Mexicans still enjoy the papayas, mangoes, and other tropical fruits known to their Indian ancestors. If they are available, fresh mangoes can be substituted for canned ones when you make mango canela.

1-pound can mangoes
¼ cup shredded coconut
1 teaspoon cinnamon

1. Chill can of mangoes overnight in the refrigerator.
2. To serve, place each mango section in a dessert dish or fruit cup, top with coconut, and sprinkle lightly with cinnamon.

Serves 4 to 6

Mango canela is a spicy and cooling treat.

Coconut Ice
Caribbean Islands

Recipe by Cheryl Davidson Kaufman

Caribbean cuisine is a particularly diverse blend of foods that reflects the tastes and traditions of the people who have come to the islands over the years from many different parts of the world. In the Caribbean, dessert is more likely to be a piece of fresh fruit than a rich chocolate concoction. The islands offer a huge variety of fruit, from pineapples and bananas to the more exotic mangoes, papayas, and custard apples. Desserts made with fruit, including different kinds of pudding, sherbet, and ice cream, are also popular. This sweet and icy coconut treat is a perfect dessert for a hot Caribbean night.

2 cups whole milk
3 cups shredded coconut, fresh or packaged
1 cup sugar
pinch of cream of tartar
1 egg yolk, beaten
a few drops almond extract

1. In a small saucepan, scald milk. Place 2 cups coconut in a sieve. Pour hot milk over coconut while holding sieve over large bowl to catch liquid. Use the back of a spoon to squeeze all of the milk out of the coconut.
2. In a large saucepan, combine coconut milk, sugar, and cream of tartar. Cook over low heat, stirring constantly, until sugar has dissolved.
3. Remove pan from heat and add beaten egg yolk. Beat well with a spoon. Stir in remaining coconut and add 2 or 3 drops almond extract. Taste and add more almond extract if desired.
4. Pour into 2 pie pans. Cover with plastic wrap and place in freezer.
5. Remove coconut ice from freezer after 4 hours and break apart with a fork. Serve immediately.

Serves 4 to 6

Banana Fritters
Caribbean Islands

Recipe by Cheryl Davidson Kaufman

2 large ripe bananas, mashed
3 tablespoons plus 1 teaspoon
**   all-purpose flour**
½ teaspoon baking powder
4 tablespoons sugar
**   dash cinnamon**
1 egg, beaten
**   vegetable oil for frying**

1. In a medium bowl, combine bananas, flour, baking powder, 2 tablespoons sugar, cinnamon, and egg and stir well.
2. Pour ½ inch of oil into a large frying pan. Heat oil over medium-high heat for about 4 or 5 minutes.
3. Carefully drop tablespoons of dough into oil and fry for 2 or 3 minutes per side or until golden brown.
4. With a slotted spoon, remove fritters from oil and drain on paper towels. Sprinkle with remaining sugar.

Makes 12 fritters

Coconut and bananas give these desserts the taste of the islands. Pictured are banana fritters (*foreground*) and coconut ice (*upper left*).

Filled Cookies/ Alfayores
Argentina

Most Argentines are of European ancestry. The Argentine diet emphasizes meat, particularly beef, and most Argentines enjoy outdoor barbecues. Afternoon tea, an English tradition, is also very popular. These delicate cookies are favorites at teatime and at special parties.

Filling:

1 14-ounce can sweetened condensed milk
1 tablespoon butter or margarine, melted
2 tablespoons lemon extract
1 cup shredded coconut

1. Fill a saucepan with enough water to cover the can of condensed milk, and bring water to a boil.
2. Submerge unopened can of condensed milk in water, reduce heat, and simmer for 3 hours.
3. Cool milk.
4. Combine milk with melted butter or margarine and lemon extract and beat until smooth. Refrigerate until ready to use.

Cookies:

½ lemon
½ cup flour
1 teaspoon baking powder
1¼ cup cornstarch
6 tablespoons butter
1 whole egg
1 egg yolk

1. Preheat oven to 350°.
2. Grate rind of lemon. Set aside.
3. Sift flour, baking powder, and cornstarch together. Set aside.
4. Cream butter and sugar until smooth. Add lemon rind, egg, and egg yolk, and continue beating.
5. Add flour mixture a little at a time and mix until dough is smooth.
6. On a lightly floured surface, roll dough to ⅛-inch thickness.

7. Using a cookie cutter or the rim of a glass, cut dough into 2-inch circles.
8. Arrange circles on baking sheet and bake at 350° for about 15 minutes.
9. Allow cookies to cool for one minute before removing from baking sheet. Cool completely on wire rack.
10. When cool, spread 1 teaspoon filling on each cookie and roll the side with topping in the coconut.
11. Place one cookie on top of another (filled sides up) to form a "sandwich."

Makes 3 dozen cookies

Milk Pudding/ Dulce de Leche
Brazil

Brazil is, by far, the largest country in South America in both area and population. Coffee is Brazil's chief drink, but Brazilians also drink fruit beverages and a tealike beverage called mate. This pudding is a favorite dessert with Brazilian children.

1 can condensed milk
½ cup whole milk
4 eggs
⅓ cup sugar
1 tablespoon water

1. With a hand mixer or in a blender, beat eggs.
2. Add condensed milk and blend well. Set aside.
3. Heat sugar over medium-high heat in a small saucepan, stirring constantly, until sugar caramelizes (turns brown).
4. Quickly pour sugar mixture into bottom of ovenproof mold or bowl, coating the bottom and sides of container.
5. Pour custard mixture into mold.
6. Bake at 350° for 45 minutes, or until a toothpick inserted in the center comes out clean.
7. When cool, turn onto platter and chill until ready to serve. Pudding will be covered with a caramel sauce.

Serves 6

A fluffy meringue topped with fruit is a refreshing dessert after a heavy meal.

Almond Meringues with Fresh Fruit
Merengues de Almendra con Frutas Frescas
Chile

Recipe by Helga Parnell

Chile, a land of great variety, is located on the southwest coast of South America. Most Chileans are of mixed Spanish and Indian ancestry, and many others are of unmixed European descent. Chileans enjoy several traditional dishes. The meringue below might be served in the homes of upperclass Chileans.

3 egg whites, at room temperature
¼ teaspoon cream of tartar
 pinch of salt
¾ cup sugar
¾ teaspoon vanilla
¾ cup freshly chopped toasted almonds
 sliced fresh fruit or berries, or well-drained canned fruit of your choice

1. Preheat the oven to 300°.
2. Cover a baking sheet with kitchen parchment paper or heavy-duty aluminum foil (dull side up).
3. Beat egg whites, cream of tartar, vanilla and salt until stiff peaks form.
4. Add the sugar, 1 tablespoon at a time, and beat well after each addition. Continue beating until the mixture, called a meringue, is stiff and glossy.
5. Gently fold in the almonds.
6. With a spoon, form 6 evenly divided mounds of meringue, about 1½ inches apart, on the lined baking sheet. Using the back of the spoon, build up the sides and make a small hollow in the center of each mound to form a nestlike shape.
7. Bake at 300° for 20 to 25 minutes.
8. Turn the oven off. Let the meringues cool in the oven. When cool, remove the foil or parchment paper from the meringues.
9. When ready to serve, clean, peel, and slice the fruit. Place the meringues on individual plates and top them with fruit.

Serves 6

Alfayores (top, far right and far left) are popular as a dessert and as a teatime snack. Milk pudding (below), which is also called flan, is a favorite dessert in many South American countries. (Recipes on pages 48 and 49.)

THE CAREFUL COOK

Whenever you cook, there are certain safety rules you must always keep in mind. Even experienced cooks follow these rules when they are in the kitchen.

1. Always wash your hands before handling food.
2. Thoroughly wash all raw vegetables and fruits to remove dirt, chemicals, and insecticides.
3. Use a cutting board when cutting up vegetables and fruits. Don't cut them up in your hand! And be sure to cut in a direction *away* from you and your fingers.
4. Long hair or loose clothing can catch fire if brought near the burners of a stove. If you have long hair, tie it back before you start cooking.
5. Turn all pot handles away from you so that you will not catch your sleeves or jewelry on them. This is especially important when younger brothers and sisters are around. They could easily knock a pot off the stove and get burned.
6. Always use a pot holder to steady hot pots or to take pans out of the oven. Don't use a wet cloth on a hot pan because the steam it produces can burn you.
7. Lift the lid of a steaming pot with the opening away from you so that you will not get burned.
8. If you get burned, hold the burn under cold running water. Do not put grease or butter on it. Cold water helps to take the heat out, but grease or butter will only keep it in.
9. If grease or cooking oil catches fire, throw baking soda or salt at the bottom of the flame to put it out. (Water will *not* put out a grease fire.) Call for help, and try to turn all the stove burners to "off."

METRIC CONVERSION CHART

WHEN YOU KNOW		MULTIPLY BY	TO FIND	
MASS (weight)				
ounces	(oz)	28.0	grams	(g)
pounds	(lb)	0.45	kilograms	(kg)
VOLUME				
teaspoons	(tsp)	5.0	milliliters	(ml)
tablespoons	(Tbsp)	15.0	milliliters	
fluid ounces	(oz)	30.0	milliliters	
cup	(c)	0.24	liters	(l)
pint	(pt)	0.47	liters	
quart	(qt)	0.95	liters	
gallon	(gal)	3.8	liters	
TEMPERATURE				
Fahrenheit	(°F)	5/9 (after subtracting 32)	Celsius	(°C)

COMMON MEASURES AND THEIR EQUIVALENTS

3 teaspoons = 1 tablespoon

8 tablespoons = ½ cup

2 cups = 1 pint

2 pints = 1 quart

4 quarts = 1 gallon

16 ounces = 1 pound

INDEX

Honey spice cake will satisfy everyone's sweet tooth. (Recipe on page 44.)

Summer pudding is a tasty dessert for any time of year. (Recipe on page 40.)

3606

641.8
DES   Desserts around the
                  world